PRAGUE

The historical section of the city, its monuments and culture

Polish

Polski – Polish name for Poland
Polach – Man from Poland
Polka – Woman from Poland

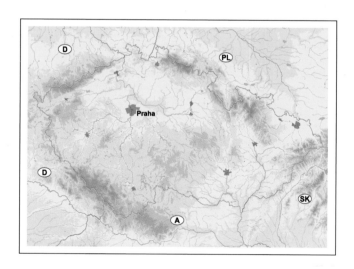

INTRODUCTION

Welcome to Prague, the capital of the Czech Republic. Prague has been fulfilling its task as the core of the country for more than 12 centuries and during that time it has grown into one of the most beautiful cities in the world. The centuries are indelibly etched into its face; it has gone through some good times and not so good times, which have left in our "Mother of Cities", as Prague is called, an unusual atmosphere that intensifies its allure. Visitors will find a rich collection of monuments that were created in the old Roman times and encompass all the subsequent styles, all the way up to the present. We would like to present both Prague's past and present in our publication. We have focused on monuments, particularly those in the historical heart of the city, which are on UNESCO's list. The text is clearly divided according to the individual sections of Prague, and monuments and places of interest are highlighted. The index and page headers will also help you to orient yourself in the text. Illustrational colour photographs, attached guide maps and other well-arranged facts about the city accompany the entire brochure. We wish you a pleasant stay and hope that the information in our publication will help you to get to know Prague better and later remind you of the pleasant times that you will surely spend here.

The editors

PRAGUE
The historical section of the city, its monuments and culture

Publisher: Unios CB, spol. s r. o.
MCU vydavatelství Unios, Hany Kvapilové 10, 370 10 České Budějovice
Tel./Fax: +420/387 428 360, e-mail: vydavatelstvi@unios.cz, www.unios.cz
Technical editors: Pavel Dvořák, Radek Eliášek, Petr Steinbauer
Text: Viktor Kubík
Photographs: Ladislav Bulva, Libor Sváček, Pavel Štecha, Radovan Boček
Maps: SHOCart Zlín
Translation: Skřivánek Translation Service – Gillian Purves
Commercial presentation: MCU vydavatelství Unios, Marek Otípka
Typesetting: Jan Kubeš
Printing: Typodesign, s. r. o., České Budějovice
Distribution: GeoClub s. r. o., www.geoclub.cz,
Prague – tel.: +420/283 890 152, fax: +420/283 890 153, e-mail: praha@geoclub.cz
Brno – tel.: +420/545 229 343, fax: +420/545 229 345, e-mail: brno@geoclub.cz
MCU Praha, s. r. o.; mcu.praha@unios.cz; tel.: +420/603/439461

1st edition, České Budějovice 2002
5th publication in the Uniosguide series, 72 pages

ISBN 80-86141-21-7
ISBN 80-86141-22-5 (angl. vyd.)

View of Lesser Town and Prague Castle across the Vltava River

" . . . I see a large city, whose fame touches the stars . . . There in the woods by the Vltava River you will find a person who is hewing the threshold (práh) of his home and in accordance with this, you will name the city Praha (Prague) . . . " In a similar manner, the legends of the prophetic, passionate mythical princess Libuše depict how she founded and named our capital city. All Czechs know this tale thanks to Kosmas, who at the beginning of the 12th century wrote an account of it in his chronicle. But only the opera by Bedřich Smetana spread the tale into public awareness. Libuše was said to have made her prophecy from Vyšehrad, the oldest mythical seat of the then princedom. As the wife of the mythic Přemysl Oráč, she became the founder of the Premyslian dynasty, which then ruled the Czech lands for more than five hundred years. In spite of Kosmas and Bedřich Smetana, everything probably happened somewhat differently. However, the history of the Czech state and the history of Prague are indivisible from each other.

"PRAGA CAPUT REI PUBLICAE"

Prague, the capital city of the Czech Republic, lies along the Vltava River, in the middle of the Czech basin. Today, around 1.2 million people live in Prague, which is about 12% of the population of our country. Its populousness and area (about 500 km^2) make it the largest city in the Czech Republic. Due to the richness and beauty of its monuments, the historical heart of Prague was placed on UNESCO's list of protected monuments in 1992. Deservedly, it is said that Prague is the most beautiful capital city in Europe. Apologies to Paris and Rome.

The populating of this location began as early as in pre-historical times. This was helped by both its location in the centre of the Czech basin and also by the suitable climatic conditions and terrain. The Vltava River has been, from time immemorial, making its way through the deposits of the cretaceous sea and its current created today's broken terrain. To this day, the Barrandov cliffs harbour the fossilised remains of trilobites and other ancient plants and animals. This majestic sarcophagus of a vanished world, together with the hillsides of Petřín, Letná and other hills of the Vltava valley protected the future heart of Prague from the cold northern and intense western winds.

These parts have been continuously populated since the 4th millennium BC, as shown by discoveries, the most important of which mainly come from the outskirts of Prague, e. g. from Šárka or from Unětice. Back then this was already a settlement that was significant for the entire Czech basin. From the Hallstatt period (from the 6th century BC) this land formed a substantial part of the Celt world. One of the oldest aristocratic Celt graves has been documented on our lands. Bohemia was a settlement for the Boii tribe, whose famous commander, Brena, during his military campaign into Italy, conquered republican Rome. Golden coins were also minted here. Not far from Prague, just past Kladno u Mšeckých Žehrovic,

Vyšehrad – sculptures with mythical personalities

a statue of a Celtic hero was found, which is considered to be one of the oldest works of Celtic art. On the outskirts of Prague, in Závist nad Zbraslaví, the ruins of a fort from the end of the 5th century BC lie at a location where in the 2nd century BC a famous opidum came into being, which was not one of the largest in area but of the Celtic structures known up to that point, it is believed to have the most massive fortifications. But not even this most magnificent fortress of the Celtic world was able to stop the Germanic people.

They took the name of this land from the Celts and, after the Boii tribe, named it Bojohémum, Bainaib, and finally Bohemia. Bohemia then became their home for the next five centuries. The Marobud's tribe of Markomans warred here with the Roman Empire, and the Langobard tribe, who so thoroughly wiped out the last remains of ancient civilization in Italy, experienced their heyday here. Even when, in the year 791, the army of Charles the Great was returning from its victorious war with the Avars, they became acquainted with Langobard mercenaries in the Frank army at the memorable place of their ancestors and mourned the abandoned grave of the famous King Wacho. It seems they lamented in the ruins in Závist nad Zbraslaví.

But at this time, the Slavs already lived here. Only with them is the emergence of Prague, in the location it is found today, connected. Even though our Slavic ancestors only came to these lands at the turn of the 5th and 6th centuries, they only settled, up to the 8th century, in the outskirts of what would become "Old Prague": in Šárka, in Bohnice, in Butovi-

Horse-mounted statue of St. Wenceslas

ce and at Levý Hradec – the oldest seat of the Premyslian dynasty. Only the growing need of the state, the significance of the local market and ford lead to the creation of Prague Castle, which served as the residence of the Czech prince only from the 9th century. Therefore, Prague castle has been the centre of the Czech state for one thousand two hundred years. Besides Papal Rome, you will not find another older centre of a state in Europe that has been continually utilised up to now.

The Premyslian Empire and Premyslian Prague proliferated together with Christianity, which was made accessible to the local people by St. Cyril and St. Methodius in the Slavic language. They came to us from Byzantium, but in Greater Moravia, where they were summoned in the year 864, they battled from the beginning with their Latin-oriented counterparts from the Frank Empire. It was as if this encounter between the Eastern and Western world at the very dawn of the Czech state marked the later peripeteias of our modern history. However, the Western orientation won out. Prince Wenceslas († 929 or 935), the principal sacred patron and eternal ruler of this land, anchored the Czech state in western politics and after the founding of Prague's bishopric (974) even Latin culture prevailed over Old Slavic. But Greater Moravia's heritage remained present, particularly in the popularity of an unusual type of cathedral in the shape of a rotunda.

Prague in the 10th century was an imposing, large metropolis. Ibrahim Ibn Jakob, the Arabian traveller and entrepreneur, described Prague as a rich "stone city". Unfortunately, not much is left from his time; the following epoch of Romanesque art was more generous. Monuments at Prague Castle, numerous temples, fragments of the Judita's stone bridge and wholly unique Romanesque city houses support the extraordinary significance and wealth of Prague in the 11th and 12th centuries. In spite of this, Prague did not have the rights of a city, and its built-up area, as isolated yards, went from Prague Castle to the Vltava River ford and further along the other side of the river all the way to the Vyšehrad fortification. The densest and richest built-up area was in the location that would later become Old Town (Staré Město), which was then called Mezihrady (between castles). There, an international market blossomed. That is also why this section became the heart of the city. King Wenceslas I, between the years 1230–41, enclosed it with ramparts and with the founding of St. Gall's town (Havelské město), laid down the foundations for the freedoms of a city. Probably from this time forward, Mezihrady came to be also known as "Prague's City" (Pražské město), after Prague Castle. At that time, the Gothic style also pervaded here: additional city buildings, palaces and cloisters were built. In the middle of the 13th century about 4,000 inhabitants lived in the Prague agglomeration, which was a large city at that time. However, by the beginning of the 14th century, the number of inhabitants of Prague rose to 10,000 people. The expansion of the capital city reflected the flowering of the Czech state. The Premyslian dynasty – after more than five hundred years on the throne – ruled from Prague not only Bohemia, Moravia and Silesia, but also the Polish and Hungarian kingdoms. The richness of the Kutná Hora silver mines evoked the same kind of fever that occurred in the 19th century in the Klondike, and the silver Prague groschen, minted from the year 1300, represented one of the most stable currencies in Europe for the next three centuries. In Olomouc, in the year 1306, the young Wenceslas III was murdered, thus the Premyslian dynasty died by the sword and the linked states immediately fell apart. However, it remained an attractive example for central Europe. The Luxemburgs

Holy Cross Rotunda

and Jagiellons imitated it, but only the Hapsburgs renewed the unity of central Europe.

The Luxemburgs ruled us for almost one hundred and thirty years (1310–1437). Jan Luxemburg, "royal diplomat" and "the last knight", acquired the Czech throne with his marriage to Eliška Přemyslovna. He sold various privileges, and so Old Town (Staré Město) was able to buy the right to have a town hall (1338) and thus become a true medieval city. Jan's son Wenceslas was raised in the Paris court, where he took the name Karel. He acquired the emperor's crown and became Charles IV (Karel IV). He did a lot for Prague, which was the capital city of the Czech state and also of the Holy Roman Empire. He had Prague Castle rebuilt, and was credited for raising Prague's bishopric to an archbishopric (1344) and with his father founded St. Vitus' Cathedral (katedrála sv. Víta). After the death of the builder, Matthias of Arras, he called from Gmünd an extraordinarily gifted young man and all-around artist, Peter Parler, who among other things built the Charles Bridge. In the

Prague groschen (beg. of the 14th century)

year 1348 he founded Charles University, the oldest university in central Europe, and that year he also laid the foundation for Prague's New Town, which displaced a number of old, scattered structures. The expansion of the fortifications under the castle, (today's Lesser Town [Malá Strana]), the construction of a number of monumental cathedrals and cloisters, together with a belt of fortifications, which drew into the city a number of vineyards, orchards and gardens, and even old Vyšehrad, changed Prague into a large metropolis, incomparable to anything in Europe as it was then. The area of Prague reached 700 hectares and the number of inhabitants rose to 40,000. After the death of Charles IV, already then called the Father of the Homeland, his son Wenceslas IV took the throne. He was as good as his father, but he had bad luck. The old world collapsed and his closest relatives, including his brother Sigmund, just complicated his situation. In Bohemia the fine art of the "beautiful style" was expanding, but in Prague, the first European reformation was also being born.

White Mountain Monument

The Czech reformation was ahead of Europe's by more than one hundred years. We paid a harsh price for this. The burning of Jan Hus at the Council of Constance (6 July 1415) made both his backers and opponents more radical. The Hussite Revolution broke out in full force. Even though the memories of the heroic battle of the Czech Utraquists and the famous victory of their leader Jan Žižka from Trocnov helped Czechs to overcome the difficult times and inspired many artistic works, the peripeteia of the civil wars, the abundant expunging crusades and the Pope's anathemas tormented this land for almost the entire 15th century. Bohemia found itself in the isolation of heretics, Prague became poor and the number of its inhabitants fell to 25,000. Our golden age had ended.

Rulers of the Jagiellon Dynasty, who wanted to guide the country out of crisis, had many great ambitions, but unfortunately far lesser abilities. Even though Prague's crafts and trade flowered, Late Gothic art adopted the Renaissance innovations. But after Vladislav II also became the Hungarian king and moved his seat to Budín (1490), the royal oligarchy fully ruled the state and the significance of Prague again declined. The tragic death of king Ludvík in the battle at Mohacs (1526) not only ended the more than half-century rule of the Jagiellons, but opened the way for the Turks into Hungary and the Hapsburgs to power.

The Hapsburgs held together the states of Austria, Bohemia and Hungary for almost four hundred years (until the year 1918). Their accession to the Czech throne was accompanied by the growing Renaissance, which was only slowly making its way through Protestant environs, so Prague was only reached by a late wave of Renaissance art – mannerism, where however it shone brightly. The great fire of Prague Castle and Lesser Town (Malá Strana) in the year 1541 did irreparable damage, however, at the same time it provided a great opportunity to apply the new style. The Renaissance palaces around Prague Castle and the Summer Castle of Queen Anna Jagiellon (from the years 1537–63) were the avant-garde of this style. Emperor Rudolf II, in the year 1584,

Mathias' Gate – changing of the guard at Prague Castle

Hradčany Square – entrance to Prague Castle

brought his residence to Prague and Rudolfine Prague became the European centre for late mannerism. The demented but art-loving Emperor Rudolf surrounded himself with capable artists, scientists, and charlatans. He rebuilt Prague Castle and its gardens; he created an extraordinary collection of art works and was compelled to give sanction to religious freedom in his empire.

With the fall of Rudolf II, religious tolerance ended. The conflict between the Protestant majority and the Catholic Hapsburgs led to

Fountain in the 2nd courtyard of Prague Castle

the Estates Uprising, which began the Thirty Years War (1618–48). The Czech Protestants lost. The Czech state lost its rights for three hundred years – it became a mere province – and the majority of Czech royalty, intellectuals and patricians emigrated. A cruel period of re-Catholicising occurred. The frenzy of war had slaughtered half of all the inhabitants of this land, and the Protestant and Catholic armies plundered the Czech kingdom and Rudolfs collections. In spite of that, even during the war, Albrecht of Wallenstein, the ambitious emperor's general, tried to uphold Rudolfs artistic tradition. His magnificent palace in Lesser Town (Malá Strana) ushered in the monumental constructions of Prague's Baroque period. The fall of Albrecht of Wallenstein and his subsequent murder (1634) ended the patronage of this magnate, but his example was not forgotten. Prague again changed its face. The co-operation of talented artists and generous sponsors fills in the second half of the 17th and the first third of the 18th centuries.

The Age of Enlightenment brought the decline of artistic power and a fall into provincialism. In spite of that, the Estates Theatre (Stavovské divadlo) was able to celebrate the success of Mozart's Don Giovanni and the

Archbishop's Palace on Hradčanské Square

house called Bertramka became a silent witness to the composers' Prague sojourn. At that time about 80,000 people lived in Prague and from that time the number of its inhabitants has been constantly rising.

The close of the "Age of Enlightenment" is closely connected with the nationalist revival. The remainder of the Czech aristocracy and the descendants of the noble White Mountain immigrants supported the emancipation of the Czech nation, its sciences and arts and its cultural and political institutions. However, the tragic manner of the definition of a nation according to its language laid down the foundations for the national split between Czech and German-speaking Czechs. Both nationalities competed with each other and the reverberations of their rivalry can still be seen in Prague today: the German Rudolfinum and State Opera as compared with the Czech National Theatre and National Museum. As we move away from that period, it is obvious that

the works of both nationalities complement each other and this competition was very useful. Even though Czech literature written in German culminated at the turn of the 19th and 20th centuries in the books of Franz Kafka, Gustav Meyring and Franz Werfel, the rift between the two ethnic groups was widening.

Artistic works of the 19th century, including Prague's Art Nouveau, complemented the Baroque face of medieval Prague, but did not change its character. In fact, even the modern trends of the beginning of the 20th century did not harm the face of old Prague. Modern art is not a heterogeneous element in this ancient city organism, as long as it is sensitively aware of its surroundings, as is shown, for instance in the cubist structures from the time before World War I. Yes, Bohemia is the only land where cubist architecture exists, and Prague is the capital of cubist architecture.

World War I led to the fall of the Hapsburg monarchy. On 28 October 1918 the Czechoslovak Republic was announced, Prague again became a real capital city and Prague Castle welcomed the president of the Republic – T. G. Masaryk, who found his architect in the prudent Josip Plečnik. In the second half of the twenties, art deco replaced functionalism. Czech functionalism and surrealism, and also the ideas found in the writing of Karel Čapek, are world-renowned ideas that represent the varied mosaic of culture between the wars. The twenty-year period of the First Republic can be considered the second golden age in our history. However, the honeymoon between Prague and Paris ended with the Munich Pact in the year 1938. Great Britain and France threw us to Hitler.

The collapse of the First Republic and the occupation by Fascist Germany again endangered the existence of the Czech-speaking majority in this land. The atrocities wrought by the Nazis made the future coexistence of Czechs and Czech Germans – 98% of whom decided to be German Germans – impossible. The liberation of the Republic and the Prague Rebellion in May 1945 meant the return of freedom. Then after the war the displacement of 2.5 million Germans ended 700 years of coexistence of both nations in our land.

After the sad Munich experience with our western allies and under the impression that the Soviet Union freed most of the State, many Czechs fell for the illusion that it is possible to unite democracy and communism. Forty percent of the votes were enough for the Communists to take over in 1948. In the following years, with a creative enthusiasm, the new rulers tried to destroy everything that reminded them of the "antiquated" times and to replace it all with new symbols. An example is the gigantic statue of Stalin on Letná Plain, which was removed back in 1961. In the year 1968, the tanks of the "friendly" nations of the Soviet Bloc crushed the efforts of the so-called Socialism with a human face. This was followed by another stage of the systematic devastation of our cultural heritage, a reminder of which is the absurdly constructed street under the National Theatre. So, probably the only useful thing that the Communist regime left behind in Prague is Prague's subway system.

The Velvet Revolution, from the 17th of November 1989, allowed us to return to a sort of

A detail of the cathedral

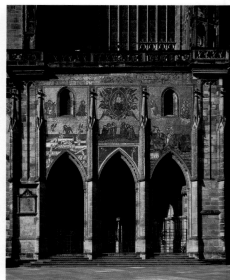

The Golden Gate with a mosaic

St. Vitus' cathedral – south entrance

Loreta

civilisation that most people in this land consider to be their own. Prague again awoke to freedom. Free elections meant the division of Czechoslovakia, because the majority of Slovaks had quite a different idea of a united state. Since 1993, Prague has been the capital city of the Czech Republic, which joined NATO on 12 March 1999 and is vehemently preparing to join the European Union.

"PRAGA MATER URBIUM"

Prague is an astonishing organism. It is not unusual to find that the Baroque façade of a building hides Gothic masonry and Romanesque basements. Old Prague is a medieval city with a Baroque overcoat, adorned with modern art like jewellery. Adjoining its historical heart (Prague Castle, Hradčany, Lesser Town, Old Town, and Vyšehrad) is the inner town, whose quarters grew from old outskirts, and from the 18th and particularly the 19th centuries they grew together with Prague towns (e.g. Karlín, Smíchov, Holešovice, Vinohrady, Vršo-

vice, Žižkov). And now the outer town is connected to them today, full of housing developments, shopping centres, family villas, forests and gardens, but also industrial units (e. g. Jižní Město, Jihozápadní Město, Bohnice, Prosek).

PRAGUE CASTLE, HRADČANY AND STRAHOV

Prague Castle has been, for more than 1200 years, the political centre of our state. Today, the president of the Republic resides there and it includes the New Palace, and the so-called **Theresa's Wings (Tereziánská křídla)**. This structure was consolidated by Niccola Pacassi in the 18th century from individual castle palaces, mainly those from the time of Rudolf II. **Matthias' Gate (Matyášova brána)**, dating from the year 1614, is a memorial to Rudolf's successor Matthias II, but **the Picture Gallery of Prague Castle** still reminds us of Rudolf's passion for art.

Today, the oldest heart of the castle mainly hosts tourists. The old, medieval **Royal Pal-**

ace harbours Romanesque basements from the 12th century and a Gothic ground floor with the **Columned Hall** of Wenceslas IV, and the late Gothic throne room **Vladislav Hall**. The throne room is the work of architect Benedikt Ried, and it replaced three original halls of the Luxemburg Palace and, in its time (1486–1502), created in Europe the largest vaulted area without interior supports (62 x 16 m). Today, the president is elected here and it hosts the most important political ceremonies. Benedikt Ried completed the late Gothic vaults and adjoining riding stairway with Renaissance windows, portals and the Renaissance Ludvík's Wing. Uniting tradition with the modernity of the day is a constant process. The architect of president T. G. Masaryk, the world renowned Josip Plečnik, carried out many alterations to the castle (1920–34), which sensitively and intelligently make the castle complex unique, and President Václav Havel with Bořek Šípek and Eva Jiřičná are trying to continue in this tradition today.

Castle Stairs from the Black Tower

The true heart of the Czech state and the most sacred place in all of the Czech lands lies in the middle of the main, third courtyard. This is **St. Vitus' Cathedral (katedrála sv.**

Evening ambience on Golden Lane

15

View of Prague Castle from Strahov

Víta), which incorporates **St. Wenceslas' Chapel (kaple sv. Václava)**. Here rests the body of the eternal ruler and protector of this land. Above his grave the **Crown Jewels** have been placed in the crown chambers. The most valuable of which, St. Wenceslas' Crown, comes from the time of Charles IV (Karel IV). St. Wenceslas' Chapel, built during Charles IV's reign by Peter Parler (completed in 1367), shows the significance of this place. Its square ground plan goes against the customary design of a cathedral ground plan at that time. The walls are covered with polished semi-precious stones and frescos, of which the part making up the St. Wenceslas legend comes from the 16th century. The two-metre-high argillite statue of St. Wenceslas (completed in 1373) and the frescos with the emperor's portrait are from the period of Charles' reign, as is the extraordinary star-vaulted chapel.

The dominating feature of the southern façade of the cathedral is the tower topped with a Renaissance gallery and a Baroque "onion" cupola. Between the large southern tower and St. Wenceslas' Chapel one can find the monumental entrance to the cathedral, called **the Golden Gate**. It is decorated with a mosaic from the time of Charles IV on which he is portrayed with his fourth wife, Elizabeth of Pommern. It was created in 1371 by Venetian mosaicists according to the design of Czech painters and up until today it is considered to be the largest and oldest outdoor mosaic north of the Alps. After its recent restoration, it is again resplendent in its former beauty. Besides St. Wenceslas Chapel and the Golden Gate with the southern tower, Parler worked on the cathedral presbytery to the **Old Sacristy**, which has a boldly vaulted ceiling with a suspended apex stone,

Singing Fountain in front of Belvedere

which for its time (1356) was quite an achievement. The **presbytery's vaulted ceiling** is also remarkable; this is one of the oldest webbed vaulted ceilings in Europe (finished in 1385).

In Prague's cathedral works, after the middle of the 14th century, a late Gothic architectural morphology was born, which about 50 years later expanded throughout all of central Europe. The fact that statue production arose from Parler's workshops is no less noteworthy. The **tombstones** of six Premyslian rulers and Bishop Jan Očko of Vlašim in the ground floor chapel, together with a wholly unique collection of **21 portrait busts on the lower triforium** and an additional **10 busts of saints on the outer triforium**, make the cathedral a magnificent tabernacle of medieval sculptures.

After the death of Peter Parler (1399), construction significantly slowed down and after the outbreak of the Hussite Wars (1420) it completely stopped. In the following one hundred years cathedrals were simply added to. The Jagiellons built a late Gothic **royal oratory** (1493) and under the Hapsburgs a royal mausoleum was created with the graves of Ferdinand I, and Ann and Maximilian II. The Baroque cathedral was decorated with the silver **tombstone of Jan Nepomucký** (1733–36). The final construction (1873–1929), which was directed by Josef Mocker (up to the

Strahov Cloister

Petřín Lookout Tower

ginal from the year 1373 (located in the National Gallery).

Among the oldest standing structures at Prague Castle is the Benedictine **Convent of St. George**. The Baroque façade of its chapel harbours a basilica from the year 920, preserved in the state it was in after its repair in the middle of the 12th century. The convent itself was founded in the year 973. It is the oldest convent in our country and it served as an educational institution for highborn girls of Czech nobility. Along its southern side descends Jiřská Street, which runs along **Rožmberk (later Lobkovic) Palace** and the Renaissance **Burgrave's Building** and heads for the **Black Tower (Černá věž)** dating from the year 1135. The Black Tower is part of the Renaissance gate, which opens in the direction of the **Old Castle Stairs**. From Jiřská Street, you can turn off into the quaint **Golden Lane (Zlatá ulička)**. Its picturesque houses are adjoined to the castle's ramparts. The towers of the ramparts are particularly noteworthy because they served as prisons. The most famous tower is **Daliborka**, in which, under the Jagiellons, Dalibor of Kozojedy, later made famous by the composer Bedřich Smetana, was imprisoned.

In the nearby surroundings of Prague castle there are various **gardens** (the Gardens on the

year 1899) and after him Kamil Hilbert, even provided an opportunity for Czech modern artists. That time is represented in the cathedral by the famous Myslbek's **tombstone of Cardinal B. Schwarzenberg** (1892–95) or the **glass case** of F. Kysela, M. Švabinský and A. Mucha. St. Vitus' is not only a metropolitan cathedral of Prague's archbishops, but also a coronation cathedral and burial place of our rulers. It was and is a tangible symbol of the Czech state and our faith, because reverence towards St. Wenceslas always united Czech Protestants and Catholics.

Adjoining the southern side is the **Old Provost's Building**, which was once the residence of the Prague bishops. On the adjoining side, in the year 1928, the J. Plečnik **granite monolith** was erected, in honour of the victims of World War I. Further on there stands a bronze replica of the **Horse-Mounted Statue of St. George** a replica of the ori-

Funicular at Petřín

Rooftops of Lesser Town

Bastion, the Paradise Gardens, the Gardens on the Ramparts, the Deer Moat and the Royal Gardens), which have been growing here since the time of Ferdinand I (since 1534). They harbour a number of Renaissance and Baroque statues from the premier artists of their time (including M.B. Braun) and no less noteworthy structures, such as for example the Renaissance **Ball Game Court** by Bonifac Wohlmut. This is the oldest walled sports building of this type in Europe (finished in 1569). However, no less interesting is the Renaissance Summer Castle of Queen Ann Jagiellon, called **Belvedere**, which Ferdinand I (1535–63) had built in the Royal Garden for his wife. The building is decorated with dozens of Renaissance reliefs with historical and courtesan themes. Water tinkles in front of the Summer Castle, spouting from the bronze **Singing Fountain** dating from the year 1564. The east side of the Royal Gardens connects directly to the Chotek's Orchards and Letná Plain).

On the opposite side, west of Prague Castle, is **Hradčany Square (Hradčanské náměstí).** There we find the magnificent courtier and church **palaces**: Lobkovic Palace (later called Schwarzenberg) with graffiti decoration (1545–63) and the Tuscan baroque palace (finished in the year 1691 by J. B. Mathey). Next to the façade of the Archbishops' Palace is a gate leading to Sternberg Palace, in which you can find part of the collection of the **National Gallery** dedicated to old European art. In the middle of the square stands the late baroque **Marian Column** from the workshop of

St. Nicholas' Cathedral

square is the oldest heart of the castle, the third Prague city, which was founded around the year 1320, but it only became a royal city in the year 1598. The smaller city buildings were pushed out by stately palaces of the aristocrats with their luxurious gardens (for example the garden of Černín Palace) and a number of cathedrals, for example the extensive **Loreta** by K. I. Dienzenhofer (1722). They particularly reflect the style of the quarter **New World (Nový svět).** Today, most feature Renaissance and early Baroque façades. With their poetic enchantment, they create a humanising antipole to the stately monumental palaces.

South of Hradčany the **Strahov Premonstratensian Cloister**, which was founded in the middle of the 12th century, spreads out. After many reconstructions, its most distinct feature is its Baroque face. The extensive buildings serve not only for the Premonstratensian Cloister but also as the **National Literature Memorial Building** and the rich **Strahov Picture Gallery**. The library here is especially noteworthy; it contains 130,000 books, 2,500 manuscripts (the oldest of which dates from the 9th century), around 1,500 in-

F. M. Brokoff (1726) and on the edge of the square, by the corner of Salmovský Palace, a **statue of T. G. Masaryk,** our first president, was unveiled in the year 2000. The

Garden of Wallenstein Palace

cunabula, and also the legacy of 1,200 Czech writers. The Strahov complex also contains charming gardens, from which there is a beautiful view of Prague.

PETŘÍN AND MALÁ STRANA

Strahov is actually a part of the **Petřín Orchards**, which are the remains of the original layout. They were gradually pushed out by vineyards and gardens. Today, a two kilometre scenic path leads along Petřín, which will lead us through the local places of interest, for example the **Petřín Lookout Tower** – a 60 m tall replica of Paris's Eiffel Tower – or the curious **Labyrinth of Mirrors**. Both were created during the Jubilee Exhibition of 1891. The **The Hunger Wall (Hladová zeď)** is the remains of the fortification of Lesser Town, which Charles IV had built after the year 1360, reputedly to employ Prague's poor. Other Petřín curiosities include the **Carpathian Church (Karpatský kostelík)** dating from the 16th century, which was brought over to today's Kinský gardens from Carpathian Velká Lúčka, and the **Funicular Railway**. On Petřín you can find many statues and sculptures, for example, Myslbek's monument to the Romantic poet K. H. Mácha (from the year 1912) – a favourite place for couples in love.

Petřín and Prague Castle embrace below them **Lesser Town (Malá Strana)**, known earlier as Smaller (Menší) and even before that New Town (Nové Město). A mercantile settlement already existed here in the 8th century, but after Prince Břetislav moved the Jewish settlers from here to the other bank of the Vltava River (in the 11th century), it became the residence of the city's Czech aristocracy and the envoys of the surrounding rulers. Even today many embassies are located here. However, the quaint **Nerudova Street**, connecting Lesser Town with Prague Castle,

Lesser Town from Rudolfinum (St. Nicholas, St. Thomas, Strahov Cloister)

Vrtbovský's Garden

shows that not only the aristocracy resided here. Lesser Town received the rights of a city from Přemysl Otakar II (1257). At that time its centre was Lesser Town Square (Malostranské náměstí) with **St. Nicholas' Church (kostel sv. Mikuláše)**, which was rebuilt by Christopher and Killian Ignatius Dienzenho-fer (1704–52). St. Nicholas' Church, together with the adjoining Jesuit dormitory, is the most monumental and most representative of Prague's Baroque religious structures. Not far from here, in Karmelitská Street, there stands a perhaps more humble but possibly more famous structure. Originally a Protest-

Lesser Town house marking

Palaces and gardens in Lesser Town

ant cathedral, after the lost uprising, it was handed over to the Catholics and consecrated as **Our Lady Victorious (Panna Marie Vítězná)**. In this, the first Baroque Church in Prague, one can find the miraculous **Infant Child of Prague (Pražské jezulátko)**, dating from the year 1628. A Baroque treasu-

re of another sort is harboured in the nearby Augustinian **Church of St. Thomas (kostel sv. Tomáše)**, for which, in the year 1636, an altar was ordered from P. P. Rubens.

The magnificence of a number of Baroque palaces located here (e.g. Thun-Hohenstein Palace on Nerudova Street by J. Santini from

Lesser Town house marking

23

the year 1726) and the charm of Baroque gardens (e. g. Vrtbovský's Garden with statues by M. B. Braun from the year 1730 or Ledeburský Garden by J. Santini from the year 1720) build upon the example of **the palace of Albrecht of Wallenstein** (1624–30), who utilised the Protestant property confiscated after the Battle of White Mountain and on the site of 22 brick buildings and several gardens built his grandiose residence. He decorated the adjoining garden with bronze statues by the famous Adrien de Vries (1626–27), but you'll only find copies of them there, because the originals, dating from the year 1648, were stolen by the Swedes. Before Albrecht of Wallenstein, these aristocratic residences were much more humble, but no less majestic, as **Smiřický Palace** on Lesser Town Square demonstrates, even though part of its façade was reconstructed after the year 1763. Incidentally, from exactly this point on 23 May 1618 a group of

Czech noblemen set out for the Castle angry because of the constant violations of religious freedom and the rights of Czech Protestants. They expressed their indignation by throwing the offending clerks out of windows. This – already the third defenestration in our history – started not only the Estates Uprising but also the Thirty Years War. Next to Smiřický Palace stands **Sternberg Palace**, in which a horrendous fire occurred (1541). The fire struck not only Lesser Town but also Prague Castle. But Lesser Town had lain in ashes before, at the beginning of the Hussite Wars (1419), when a mob "celebrated" the death of Wenceslas IV. Of the oldest structures that have survived to today, probably the most impressive is the Knights of St. John **Church of the Virgin Mary Under the Chain (kostel Panny Marie pod řetězem)** (1169). The Knights of St. John (after 1530 the Knights of Malta) were to have protected the stone bridge.

Smiřický palace on Lesser Town Square

Charles Bridge

CHARLES BRIDGE, THE VLTAVA RIVER, PRAGUE'S BRIDGES AND ISLANDS

Prague has had its own stone bridge since 1169. Back then it was named **Judith's bridge**, after the wife of King Vladislav I. It stood approximately in the same location as today's Charles Bridge, but it was lower, it had more arches and it was longer, because from the Lesser Town bank it headed more along the flow of the river. Up to today, the **Lesser Town Bridge Gate (Malostranská mostecká brána)** indicates the axis of Judith's Bridge, which was swept away by a flood in 1342. In the year 1357 Charles IV gave instructions to start building a new stone bridge, named **Charles Bridge (Karlův most)**. It still stands today thanks to its outstanding construction, for which the genius of Peter Parler is probably responsible. It is 520 m long, 10 m wide and is supported by 16 arches. The bridge's pillars became pedestals for decorative statues. Now, 28 statues by the best sculptors of their time decorate the bridge. The oldest preserved statue is St. Jan Nepomucký by Jan Brokoff (1683). It is erected at the location from where his body was thrown into the river. A cult dedicated to this saint spread from here, as did the custom of placing his statues on bridges. Here the orders of the church and the faculties of the university competed with one another for the glorification of their saints. The artists who worked for them even included M. B. Braun (for example the statue of St. Lutigarde from the year 1710) and F. M. Brokoff (the most famous are the Holy Trinity from the year 1714). On the other side of the bridge stands the **Old Town Bridge Tower (Staroměstská mostecká věž)**, richly decorated with sculptures from the 1380s. The ruling Charles IV, his son Wenceslas IV, and the land

Old Town bridge tower

they rule are under the symbolic protection of earthly saints.

If we return to the Lesser Town bank, we can visit the small, but picturesque, **Kampa Island**. Like Lesser Town, it is also full of splendid palaces, beautiful gardens and parks, and also romantic secluded areas where ghostly spirits, known from old Prague fairy-tales, hide.

The riverbanks in Prague are connected by a total of 17 bridges. The oldest and most famous, Charles Bridge, forms a part of the Royal Route (Královská cesta), while the newest, **Barrandov Bridge** (built in the years 1978–88) is part of Prague's south highway bypass. The highest, the **Nusle Bridge** extends above the Nusle Valley at a height of 43 m.

There are eight islands on the Prague section of the Vltava River. Besides Kampa Island, **Slavonic Island (Slovanský ostrov)** (up to the year 1918 called Žofín) is another centre of social life. Concerts and balls have been held

St. Jan Nepomucký

A cruise ship on the Vltava River at Čech's Bridge

Kampa Island, view of Čertovka

in the restaurant since 1830. Among others, F. Liszt, H. Berlioz and P. I. Tchaikovsky gave concerts here. One can soak up the atmosphere of the Vltava River during a cruise on a riverboat. The more able bodied can rent a small boat and savour, up close, the romantic atmosphere between Prague's weirs. But one must be careful, the average depth of the Vltava riverbed is around 2.5 metres and the most well known of Prague's mystical creatures, water sprites, may be lurking nearby!

THE OLD TOWN
AND THE JEWISH GHETTO

Old Town (Staré Město) is the oldest and richest Prague quarter. Its inception is connected with an international market, which functioned here from at least the 9th century. The adulation of Ibrahim Ibn Jakob, the Arabian merchant who passed through here in the 10th century, pertained to this part of Prague. In the area around the Old Town Square (Staroměstské náměstí) and along the main

Old Town routes, the oldest **Romanesque stone buildings** are preserved, which is wholly unique in central Europe. Today, more than seventy are known. Back when they were built the Old Town was called Mezihrady ([between castles] i.e. between Prague Castle and Vyšehrad) and an international market flourished on the present day **Old Town Square**. In the location where the Prague meridian now passes through the square, Marian's Column once stood (from the year 1680), which at the same time served as the gnomon of a sundial. It was destroyed during the declaration of the Republic in 1918. However, at this time the **Monument to Jan Hus,** founder of the Czech reformation, created by Art Noveau sculptor L. Šaloun (1915), already stood on the Old Town Square. By his side stands one of the most beautiful Prague rococo structures – **the Goltz-Kinský Palace** by A. Lurago (1755–65), built according to the project of K. I. Dienzenhofer. Today, the **National Gallery's Graphic collections** are placed here.

Medieval Prague was very cosmopolitan. To the north and northeast German entrepreneurs resided, to the south and southeast merchants from Latin countries, to the east of the square Czechs and to the northwest Jews. The oldest municipal and monarch's structures are located in the eastern part of the square. Next to the Romanesque stone **House at the Bell (dům U Zvonu),** which was rebuilt in the Gothic style and in which many medieval monarchs resided, stands the quaint **Týn School** with an arcade from the 13th century. Behind it stands the city's main cathedral, the **Cathedral of Our Lady before Týn (chrám Panny Marie před Týnem),** a large part of which was created in the 14th century by the workshop of Peter Parler. The extraordinary medieval sculptor's ornamentation was preserved along with the tombstone of Rudolf's astronomer Tycho de Brahe and a collection of the painter's work.

Memorable Celetná Street leads through this part of the Old Town, featuring the most noteworthy Old Town palaces; on the corner of the Old Town Square you'll find the **Štorch House (Štorchův dům),** with frescos of Mikoláš Aleš in a style uniting Art Nouveau with the New Renaissance tradition of nationalist revival. In the middle of Celetná Street, on the corner of the Fruit Market (Ovocný trh), stands the majestic jewel of modern architecture – the cubist **House of the Black Madonna (dům u Černé matky Boží)** by Josef Gočár (1909–11), while the Fruit Market is dominated by the classicist **Estates Theatre (Stavovské divadlo)** building, which was, among other things, witness to the famous premier of Mozart's Don Giovanni (1787). Adjoining the theatre is the **Karolinum,** a mixed complex of university buildings and a block of houses that go all the way to Celetná Street. They are mostly covered by Baroque and 19th century façades, but many interiors are Gothic. The heart of the entire complex is the Rothlév House (Rothlévův dům), which Wenceslas IV donated to the university (1383). The university rector's office has been based here since the year 1611. Even the latest renovations have not destroyed the mixed nature of this organism.

A view of the Old Town from the Lesser Town

Old Town Square, the tower of the Cathedral of Our Lady before Týn

Celetná Street connects the main square with the Late Gothic **Powder Tower (Prašná brána)** by M. Rejsek (after the year 1475). The Powder Tower is closely adjoined by the Royal Courtyard. It was a favourite private residence of Czech rulers, however, it was not preserved because it was rebuilt into the **Municipal House (Obecní dům)**, which is the most impressive palace of Art Nouveau Prague (1906–11). It was built by A. Balšánek and O. Polívka and the ornamentation was done jointly, chiefly by painter J. Preissler and sculptors Stanislav Sucharda and Ladislav Šaloun.

On the opposite, west side of the Old Town Square stands the remainder of the **town hall** with a chapel and tower dating from the 14th century. In front of the town hall, on the pavement, there is a cross commemorating the execution of 27 leaders of the tragic Estates Uprising in the years 1618–21. The building of the local government itself was created from several city houses that the municipality gradually connected from the year 1338, when

Old Town Hall – the Astronomical Clock

it received the right to build a town hall. The southern side of the town hall's façade is decorated with the still functioning **Astronomical Clock (Orloj)**, which was created by Mikuláš of Kadaň (1410) and was perfected by Master Hanuš (1490). In the year 1864, Josef Mánes created the Astronomical Clock calendar panel. From this side the town hall is also interesting due to its Late Gothic portal by M. Rejsek (1475) and on the corner the Renaissance **Minuta House (Dům U Minuty)**.

From the northern side of the square, the view opens up onto **St. Nicholas' Cathedral (chrám sv. Mikuláše)**, which was built by K. I. Dienzenhofer (1732–35). Behind the cathedral, the Jewish ghetto, which has been demolished since 1896, spreads out. The features that were preserved include the **Old-New Synagogue (Staronová synagoga)** from the 13th century, which is the oldest preserved and still functioning synagogue in central Europe, and the wholly extraordinary **Old Jewish Cemetery**, utilised from the 15th to the 18th centuries. Among the 20,000 tombstones is the grave of the famous Rabbi Löw, who in Rudolf's time was reputed to have created the

Štorch House

House of the Black Madonna

mythic Golem, an artificial person, of which, however, the rabbi lost control. The golem had to be "turned off" and hidden in an unknown location. However, most of the Jewish city underwent Art Nouveau reconstruction. **Pařížská ulice (Paris Street)**, in particular, became a manifestation of the new style, but the riverbank outskirts of the ghetto were rebuilt even sooner. Proof of this is, for example, the **Rudolfinum**. It is a sanctuary of music and artistic creation from the year 1883. It was built for the German inhabitants of Prague by the main architects of the Czech National Theatre – Josef Zítek and Josef Schulz.

The Jewish Quarter was then enclosed on the eastern side by cloisters and parish churches. From the beginning of the 13th century, about thirty in total were built in the Old Town, the most famous of which is probably **St. Agnes' Convent**, which was founded by

Anežka Přemyslova (1234) for Franciscans and Poor Clare nuns. Anežka, a sister of King Wenceslas I, was only canonized in the year 1989, but for Czechs she became a sacred guardian immediately after her death (1282). Today the National Gallery's collection of medieval art is on display in the convent.

Saint Agnes of Bohemia also founded the only Czech church order – the Order of the Cross with the Red Star, which had its headquarters alongside the Old Town Bridge Tower at the foot of Charles Bridge. The order's **St. Francis' Cathedral** was rebuilt in the Baroque style by Jean-Baptiste Mathey (1689). Thus one of the most beautiful Prague Baroque churches was created. This area, west and southwest from the Old Town Square, harbours many treasures. Through here leads the coronation route of Czech kings, which connected Vyšehrad with Prague castle; here one can find (on Karolina Světlá Street) the **Holy Cross Romanesque Rotunda (rotunda sv. Kříže)** from the 11th century, and even the famous **Bethlehem chapel (Betlémská kaple)** stood here, a place where the reformer master Jan Hus preached. It was reconstructed (1950–53) according to the demolished original from the year 1391. But this part of town was also the focal point of Catholicism, because on the Cross Square (Křížovnické náměstí) from the year 1556 the Jesuit Hall was in operation here, which, particularly after the Thirty Years War, grew into an extensive complex. Named after St. Clement's Cathedral, it is called **Klementinum**. Part of it consists of **St. Salvador's Church (kostel sv. Salvatora)**, which is connected to the socalled **Italian Chapel (Vlašská kaple)**. This is the oldest European cathedral built with an elliptical ground plan. It dates from the years

Karolinum – Gothic oriel

The Estate Theatre at the Fruit Market (Ovocný trh)

Municipal House (Obecní dům) – typical Prague Art Nouveau structure

1590–97, but it is not possible to determine its creator. What the architects in Italy only dreamed of, their Italian colleagues realised on the Prague courtyard of Rudolf II. Klementinum harbours other treasures. The Baroque-fashioned interior of the cathedral, the **Mirrored**

St. Agnes' Convent

Chapel (Zrcadlová kaple) (1724) and the **Library and Mathematical Hall** (1727–30) illustrate the development of Baroque art in Bohemia. Besides this, the Klementinum also served as a university library. Today's National Library builds on this tradition. It keeps about six million volumes with a yearly growth of around 80,000 titles and many magnificent medieval manuscripts.

To the south of Old Town Square Wenceslas I founded (1232–34) **St. Gall's Town (Havelské město)**. This was supposed to be an isolated new market, but its privileges soon extended to the old settlements. St. Gall's town became the main city market (from the coal to the fruit market) and it functions as a market to this day. In fact, New Town is connected to Old Town here, via the market.

NEW TOWN AND VYŠEHRAD

The **New Town (Nové Město)** was founded by Charles IV in the year 1348, but many of its sections were settled from as early as the 10th century, for example, Poříčí, Chudobice,

Powder Gate (Prašná brána) from Celetná Street

Old-New Synagogue

Opatovice, Rybníček, Zderaz, Podskalí and Psáře. Compared to the cosmopolitan, university and business oriented Old Town the New Town was settled by the Czech middle class, and mainly craftsmen. In fact, some crafts were relocated from Old Town to New Town so that they wouldn't disturb its luxurious character. The New Town, as outlined by the fortification of Charles IV, encompassed 360 hectares. In places, its up to 27-metre-wide streets were suitable for transportation up to the second half of the 20th century and

The Rudolfinum building at Jan Palach Square

they impressed order on the previously chaotic scattering of settlements.

On the northern side, a new development was built upon the old settlement of German merchants in the area around the Romanesque **Church of St. Peter (kostel sv. Petra)** from the 12th century, which was rebuilt into the Gothic style in the 14th and 15th centuries, and after that even a Renaissance bell tower was added. Peter's settlement (Petrská osada) was, from ancient times, called Poříčí and the main street was named after it – **Na Poříčí**. Today it is ornamented by, for example, the cubist **Legiobank Building** by Josef Gočár (1921–23). You can also find here the functionalist **Brouk and Babka department store** dating from the end of the 1930s (later renamed White Swan [Bílá labuť]). After the tearing down of the Old Town's ramparts in the 1780s, an encircling representative avenue was

built on the location of the filled in rampart moats (divided into three streets, now Revoluční, Na Příkopě and Národní), which at **Republic Square (náměstí Republiky)** connects with Na Poříčí Street. The dominant features of Republic Square are not only the Municipal House and the Powder Tower, but also **dům U Hybernů (Hibernian House** – an empire style customs house structure, named after the local Irish Franciscan monastery).

A dominant feature of Národní třída (National Avenue) and the riverbank is the famous **National Theatre**. It was built using money collected from generous citizens of the city and common people. The building was created by Josef Zítek and after the fire in 1881 it was repaired by Josef Schulz. The ornamentation was done mainly by artists of the then upcoming generation, which was even named after the National Theatre. The most famous

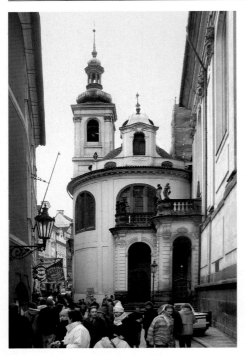

Italian Chapel (Vlašská kaple)

Today, this riverbank avenue is frequented by a lot of traffic; however, the main routes of traffic lead elsewhere. But even today, this street is very alive. The main traffic route leads from Peter's Quarter (Petrská čtvrť) to the newly built parochial **Church of St. Henry (kostel sv. Jindřicha)**. This noteworthy, and for the time of Charles IV typical, three-nave church was partially redone in the Gothic style in the 19th century. The parochial church gave its name to Jindřišská Street, which leads to the Horse Market (Koňský trh), from the year 1848 called **Wenceslas Square (Václavské náměstí)**. Wenceslas Square became, from the second half of the 19th century, the main centre of modern Prague. Its magnificent medieval dimensions (the occupied area is 41,400 m²) fully satisfy even today's needs. The exemplary buildings and palaces of Wenceslas Square can serve as an illustration of the development of our New Age architecture, but its dominant feature is the **National Museum** building. It was built by Josef Schulz between the years 1885–90, and the sculptural ornamentation (with an emblem of Bohemia

of which was notably the sculptor J. V. Myslbek, and painters M. Aleš, V. Brožík and V. Hynais. The neo-Renaissance style gradually transformed into Art Nouveau. From the very beginning, the National Theatre was built as an expression of something that represented the nation. In sight of the National Theatre, on the opposite bank of Slavonic Island (Slovanský ostrov), stands the **Waterworks Tower** dating from the end of the 15th century, which was drawn into the modern building of artistic associations known as **Mánes**. This original joining of Late Gothic and functionalism was carried out by O. Novotný (1927–30). Further along the riverbank, against the current of the Vltava River, the noteworthy **Dancing House (Tančící dům)** was recently erected (1990–96), with which Vlado Milunić and Frank O. Gehry brought into Prague a breath of the current, creative architectural thinking.

Bethlehem Chapel (Betlémská kaple)

The Dancing House (Tančící dům) at the corner of Resslova Street

The Old Town waterworks tower and the Mánes building

and Bohemian rivers at its entrance way) was created by Antonín Wagner. Even at the time of its creation, this atypical Prague Neo-Renaissance structure was not supposed to be only a museum but also a centre for Czech sciences and a representation of the cultural and political ambitions of Czech society. The spectacular interior not only harbours rich collections but also the Pantheon – a hall devoted to the commemoration of extraordinary Czech individuals.

The National Theatre

The New Town Hall on Charles Square (Karlovo náměstí)

The **Horse-Mounted Statue of St. Wenceslas** was built between the years 1912–24, in front of the National Theatre on Wenceslas Square. But, from the year 1680, his Baroque predecessor, now in the Lapidarium, stood here.

The founder of modern Czech sculpture, J. V. Myslbek, created the present-day statue. The main guardian of our land and our eternal leader is accompanied by the national patrons St. Ludmila, St. Procopius, St. Agnes of Bohe-

Night life on Wenceslas Square

The Rotunda of St. Longin

mia and St. Adalbert. Prague inhabitants use this monument as a meeting point. It doesn't matter if the meeting is a lovers' rendezvous or a political demonstration, the monument to St. Wenceslas on Wenceslas Square acts as a magnet. Our most recent history also unfolded here. All of the most important demonstrations against communism took place here.

From Wenceslas Square we will walk down Vodičkova Street directly to the former livestock market, now **Charles Square (Karlovo náměstí)**, the second main focal point of New Town. Charles IV founded it as the main centre of Prague's new side. That is why it has an unbelievable area (80,500 m²) and that is why the **New Town Hall**, which served its purpose up to the year 1784, is located here. The Town Hall building was built between the years of 1377–1418, and the corner tower in the years 1452–56. These walls were witness to the first Czech defenestration (1419), which released the avalanche of Hussite Wars. In about the middle of the east side of the square we can find the monumental Baroque **Ca-**

The National Museum building at the top of Wenceslas Square

thedral of St. Ignatius (chrám sv. Ignáce) (completed in 1670 by Carlo Lurago). Further to the east, on the corner of Štěpánská Street and Na Rybníčku Street, there stands the Romanesque **Rotunda of St. Longin** from the 11th century, which was the parochial church of the then settlement of Rybníček.

Many noteworthy monuments can be found south of Charles Square (Karlovo náměstí) in New Town. **The Emaus Monastery (Emauzský klášter)**, founded in the year 1347, is the only new structure whose completion (1372) Charles IV lived to see. He paid careful attention to its ornamentation. The beautiful three-nave hall is complemented by an extraordinary series of frescos in the cloister. This is the largest preserved collection of medieval wall paintings outside of Italy. The cloister was damaged during bombing at the close of World War II, and so its rebuilding was conducted by F. M. Černý (1967). The bold structure became the new dominant feature of this part of the riverbank. On the square stands an astonishing eight-sided cathedral of Augustinian canons, the sacred **Virgin Mary and Charlemagne**. Charles IV wanted to remind people of the Aachen chapel of Charlemagne, whose successor he considered himself to be. However, today the cupola is of a Renaissance style (1575). Its massive star vaults are purposely reminiscent of the distant past. The historicism of Gothic continued in the historicism of Renaissance.

A view from Vyšehrad down into the Vltava River valley

The medieval street plan of New Town looks almost unbelievable. This is a far-sighted urban planning concept that was ahead of its time by many centuries. We will never find out who was the author – Peter Parler, or Charles IV, or both together? Besides the extraordinary composition of the newly founded sections of town, no less noteworthy is the manner of linking these newly built up areas with the older settled areas.

Vyšehrad, the mythical seat of the Premyslian princedom, dates from the 10th century. It may be younger than Prague Castle but that takes nothing away from its significance. It reached its greatest splendour in the 2nd half of the 11th century. At that time, the castle often hosted king Vratislav II, who founded the local **Capitular Church of SS Peter and Paul (kapitulní kostle sv. Petra a Pavla).**

Its contemporary appearance is due to its remodelling in the Gothic style in the 19th century. Not far from here stands a monument to Vratislav II –**The Rotunda of St. Martin (rotunda sv. Martina).** This is the oldest preserved Prague rotunda. After the death of Vratislav II, Vyšehrad changed into mainly a ruler's fortress above Prague and remained so for 800 years. But in the 14th century Charles IV gave Vyšehrad a special sparkle when he placed it in his coronation series. From here a ruler set out on a ceremonial and symbolic pilgrimage through the city and only then could he be crowned in the cathedral with St. Wenceslas' Crown and become the Czech king. When, in the year 1866, Vyšehrad even lost its function as fortress, the local **Vyšehrad Cemetery** began to expand and change to **Slavín Cemetery**, which was, between the years

SS Peter and Paul Cathedral in Vyšehrad with a cubist residence in the foreground

The tombstone of Antonín Dvořák

1890–1902, architecturally reorganised by Antonín Wiehl. Thus the famous cemetery and memorial for the most noteworthy individuals of our land came into being. Those buried here include, for example, the authors J. Zeyer, J. Vrchlický, and K. Čapek, painters A. Mucha, and V. Špála, sculptors J. V. Myslbek and L. Šaloun, architect Josef Gočár and K. Hilbert, the composer Dvořák and the singer E. Destinnová, the politician F. L. Rieger and many others. The **Vyšehrad Gardens** were created from the ruins. To this day, one can see **the remains of the Gothic Luxemburg Palace**. After the year 1947, the Myslbek sculpture from Palacký Bridge was placed here. The mythical personalities of our past allegorically come to life here: Lumír and Píseň (1888), Přemysl and Libuše (1889), Ctirad and Šárka (1895) and Záboj and Slavoj (1892).

SMÍCHOV AND ZBRASLAV

On the opposite bank of the Vltava River lies **Smíchov**, which runs along the river all the

Bertramka – where W. A. Mozart stayed when he was in Prague

Zbraslav

way to Petřín and Lesser Town. It entered into history as a suburb of Prague during the reign of Wenceslas II, who, in the year 1297, held a magnificent coronation banquet for, according to the chronicles of that time, 190,000 noble guests and their entourage. Up to the 19th century, it was only sparsely settled along the route leading to Zbraslav and Pilsen. Bourgeoisie and noble farmsteads (Bertramka, Šmukýřka) came into being here and later even summer castles. The Renaissance **Lesser Town Waterworks Tower** (1562) is one of the older preserved monuments on the banks of the Vltava River, on Petržilkovský Island. Today, the local park is arranged as a children's playground. Not far away, but farther from the riverbank, the Baroque summer castle, known as **Portheimka** or **Buquoyka** still stands. It was built in the year 1725 by K. I. Dienzenhofer and its interiors were frescoed by V. V. Reiner. The co-

operation of these two outstanding artists created one of the most beautiful Czech Late Baroque monuments. The gardens that once belonged to the estate reached all the way to the Vltava River and in the year 1775 became the basis for today's botanical gardens. Nearby at Portheimka, after the year 1884, Antonín Barvitie built the neo-Renaissance **Church of St. Wenceslas (kostel sv. Václava)**. This illustrates the rise of Smíchov in the 19th century, when it became an industrial sector. Today, its centre is **the Anděl (Angel) Crossroads**, where the most modern buildings are now being built and are meeting the remains of classicist structures. The crossroads are dominated by the business and administrative **Zlatý anděl (Golden Angel) Centre**, which was created from glass and aluminium by Jean Nouvelle from 1996–2000. Above Smíchov, which is an industrial, workers and business district, one

Břevnov Monastery Church of St. Margaret

can find **Barrandov Cliffs**, in which at the beginning of the 19th century, Joachim Barrande found a number of noteworthy animal fossils. The illustrious **film studios** are located there and in 1927 the **lookout restaurant** came into being. One can find the famous **Bertramka** in these parts – a 17th century residence that was rebuilt in the middle of the 18th century and even hosted W. A. Mozart. He lived here with his friends, the pianists F. X. Dušek and his wife Josefína, and even composed some of his works. Today in Bertramka, one can find the museum of W. A. Mozart and the Dušeks. Concerts are held in the building and adjoining garden.

Farther south, on the left bank of the Vltava River, lies **Zbraslav**. The famous Gothic **Cistercian Cloister**, which was supposed to function as the burial place for Czech kings, stood here. It was totally destroyed at the beginning of the Hussite Wars. The current Baroque version of the cloister was worked on by J. Santini, K. I. Dienzenhofer and V. V. Reiner. Today, the complex, with its adjoining park, is an oasis of calm and it houses the **Asian Art collections of the National Gallery**. Above Zbraslav, on the other bank of the Vltava River – **Na Závisti** there is evidence of an ancient **Celtic Fortress**, whose 170 hectares was surrounded by 9 km of complex ramparts.

BŘEVNOV AND BÍLÁ HORA (WHITE MOUNTAIN)

Forested, and later agriculturally worked land spreads out to the west and northeast of Prague Castle. To the west of Hradčany, **Břevnov** was first settled. The bishop St. Adalbert founded, in 993, the oldest Benedictine monastery in Bohemia here. All that was preserved from the original structure is the impressive **Romanesque crypt** from the 11th century; however, most of the monastery buildings were remodelled at the beginning of the 18th century in the Baroque style. The **Convent Church of St. Margaret (klášterní kostel sv. Markéty)** and the **convent complex** as a whole preserved many Baroque art treasures. West of Břevnov, the remains of the local game preserve can be found. The **Hvězda Game Reserve** was founded by Ferdinand I (1534) and up until the beginning of the 19th century, forest animals were kept here; after that the reserve was transformed into a park. The name of the reserve determined the appearance of the current version of the local **Hvězda (Star) Summer Castle**. It was designed in 1555 by Ferdinand of Tirolen and the structure is actually built on the groundplan of a six-pointed star. Not far from Hvězda, we find **Bílá hora (White Mountain)**, a symbol of tragedy for most Czechs. The **Monument** is a reminder of the place where on the 8th of November 1620, the better paid emperor's Catholic League mercenary army met with the poorly paid Czech Protestant army mercenaries. Confusion, chaos and an embarrassing stampede are an apt characterisation of the professional army. For the next 300 years the Czech lands became only a Habsburg province. The elite of the land emigrated, and most of the Czech nobles, the richest from the city and the intellectuals, including the famous "teacher of the nation" J. A. Komenský disappeared. 90 % of the inhabitants of Bohemia were Protestants; those who refused to convert to Catholicism had to leave and their property was confiscated. By

Hvězda Summer Castle not far from Bílá hora (White Mountain)

Prague bridges from Letná

the end of the Thirty Years War the Czech kingdom had lost half its population. However, Bílá hora became a place of pilgrimage for Catholics. The **Cathedral of the Virgin Mary (chrám Panny Marie)**, located here, was built at the beginning of the 18th century and is decorated with the rich frescos of K. D. Asam and V. V. Reiner.

DEJVICE, LETNÁ, HOLEŠOVICE AND TROJA

Dejvice lies to the north of Hradčany and Prague Castle itself. It was mentioned in references as early as in the year 1088 and for a long time it retained its rural character. The agricultural yards were replaced by a residential suburb. In the 1930s, the **Baba residential colony** came into being here. It was organised according to the regulatory project of Pavel Janák. The treasures of functionalist architecture come from a whole parade of the foremost architects of the First Republic (J. Gočár, J. Krejcar, A. Beneš, J. Gillar and others.).

Bubeneč adjoins Dejvice in the east. The **Stromovka Royal Game Reserve** extends from here. Jan Luxemburg used it as a game reserve in 1320. Rudolf II, at the beginning of the 17th century, had ponds and galleries built here. From 1804, the vice-regent count Chotek made it accessible to the public and the game hunting castle of Vladislav Jagiellon and Rudolf II was converted by Jiří Fischer into the neo-Gothic **Vice-regent's Summer Castle**. After the year 1845, the game reserve began its transformation into an English park. Today, this romantic oasis is a protected natural monument. The **Prague Exhibition Grounds (Výstaviště Praha)** adjoin Stromovka to the east. From the end of the 19th century, these grounds served not only as a location for exhibitions and fairs but also as an entertainment centre. The famous Matthew's Fair was relocated here, but one can also find a covered pool, stadiums, theatres, cinemas, the **National Museum's Lapidarium** and many other sport and entertainment attractions. The local

The Industrial Palace at Výstaviště (the exhibition grounds)

structures that came into being for the Jubilee Exhibition of 1891 are noteworthy. The combination of the historical style of iron and glass is an interesting display of 19th century art. And, on the other hand, Křižík's Fountain, which was renewed for the Jubilee Exhibition of 1991, is a contemporary creation. The Planetarium and small pavilion adjoin the Exhibition Grounds and harbour the astonishing **Panorama of the Battle at Lipany**, which was painted by Luděk Marold (1898). The tableau and props take the viewer right into the middle of the turmoil of war in 1434.

Stromovka is bordered by the Vltava River to the north, Holešovice to the east, and from the south by a narrow band of blocks of houses, which separate it from Letná Plain. On its outskirts stands the **National Technical Museum**, whose rich collections entice lovers of antique vehicles and technical achievements from all time periods. The Letná Gardens lie on Letná Plain, which directly connect to the Chotek Orchards under the Royal Gardens under Prague Castle. Today, they

are connected by the Footbridge across Chotek's Road (Lávka nad Chotkovou silnicí), reconfigured in 1995 by the architect Bořek Šípek. So, Prague Castle actually retained a significant part of its original character. Besides the calming greenery, sports grounds and garden restaurants, one can find artistic works here, e.g. the Art Nouveau **Hanavský Pavilion** from the Jubilee Exhibition of 1891, which was moved here after 1898 or the beautiful **Prague Lookout Restaurant (Vyhlídková restaurace Praha)** from the famous Expo 1958 international exposition in Brussels. The restaurant, for its time a preeminent work (of J. Hrubý, Z. Pokorný and F. Cubr), underwent a recent reconstruction.

The communist regime had serious plans for Letná. In the 50s, the **Letná Tunnel** was built under Letná Plain, connecting Letná with the Old Town, and above it, a colossal statue of J. V. Stalin and his co-fighters. Soon after its completion, the no-easier task of demolition began, because time showed the contemptible practices of the acclaimed. Eventu-

The functionalist structure of the Veletržní palác in Holešovice

The Baroque Castle at Troja

ally, time even swept away the socialist era. During the Velvet Revolution, there was a general strike demonstration in which half a million people participated. That was the final straw that brought down the old regime. The **Chronometer** was placed where Stalin once stood – a symbol of new times.

The border dividing Letná and **Holešovice** runs between the exhibition grounds and the east end of Letná Gardens. Formerly a fishing settlement, Bubny grew together with royal Holešovice and from the 19th century changed into an industrial sector. Modern times saw it flourishing. The factories here receded to the other bank of the Vltava River and Holešovice became primarily a residential area. Neo-Renaissance and Art Nouveau structures complement functionalist gems, such as, for instance, the famous **Veletržní palác (Trade Fair Palace)** (built between the years of 1925–28).

Holešovice, Letná and Stromovka are encircled by the Vltava River, so they form a sort of peninsula. North of this peninsula lies **Troja**. Originally, this orchard was named Ovenec, but the magnificent **Sternberg Castle of Troja** meant these parts were renamed. Jean-Baptiste Mathey built this summer retreat for Václav Vojtěch of Sternberg between the years of 1679–85. Today, the Baroque interiors and gardens serve the Gallery of Prague. Below the castle lie the **Botanical Gardens**, founded in 1969 and, next to the castle, are the 45-hectare **Zoological Gardens**, which were opened to visitors in 1931. Their uniqueness lies not only in their copious utilisation of the richness and contours of the local countryside, but also in the successful keeping of Przewalski's horses. This type of horse can no longer be found in the wild and is actually an animal from ancient times.

LIBEŇ, VYSOČANY, KARLÍN, ŽIŽKOV AND VINOHRADY

On the right bank of the Vltava River and south from Troja along New Town lie the city

The metronome in Letná

quarters of Libeň, Vysočany and Karlín, which gradually changed from Romanesque and Gothic settlements to summer castles and agricultural farmsteads on the outskirts of the city until the 19th century fully drew them in as industrial and residential suburbs.

Karlín is a slightly different case. Up until 1817, vegetable gardens prospered here, along with the renowned Schönfeld Summer Castle of Růžodol, in which theatre was conducted in Czech, from the 18th century. **Invalidovna** was a former structure that was preserved. The year 1817 changed everything. Then, the spirit of classicist urban planning of the outskirts of Karlín was laid, named after Karolína Augusta, the wife of František I. Soon the **Empire style Apartment Buildings** sprang up here, part of which are preserved to this day. Karlín was the most modern part of Prague. The first gas works arose here; they provided public lighting, which spread throughout Prague and the first Prague trams ran here too. The buildings of the

local manufacturers and factories, which no longer function, were threatened with demolition and with that the demise of the whole character of the area loomed, but in 1999 **Karlín Palace** and in 2001 **Corso Karlín** were completed. The famed Riccardo Beaufil hung the current structure of glass and steel on old factory walls and an object by David Černý has brought the building to life in an original way. Thus in the old centre, Karlín Square, was renewed.

On the southern side of Karlín lies the forested hillside of **Žižkov** and under its southern slope lies the city quarter of the same name, which further to the south changes into **Vinohrady**. In the middle ages, this area was covered with vineyards, among which estates and summer castles later arose. But all was not always peaceful. On the top of Žižkov, formerly Vítkov, the siege of Hussite Prague was broken in 1420 and the vast one-hundred-dred-thousand-strong crusade army of King Sigmund Luxemburg panicked and fled. This great triumph of the Hussite Wars is commemorated by the **National Liberation Monument at Vítkov** (1929–32). In the years 1931-41, Bohumil Kafka created the monumental **Bronze Statue of Jan Žižka**, the victorious leader of the Hussites, for Vítkov. In its time, this was the largest bronze statue of a horse and rider in the world (its height and length is over 9 m and it weighs almost 17 tonnes). Besides acting as a reminder of the Hussite victory, it was supposed to commemorate the Czechoslovakian legion from the 1st World War, similarly to today's **Museum of Revolts and the Military** under Vítkov. Tourists can get an unforgettable view of Prague from here.

During the horrendous plague in the year 1680, the Plague Cemetery came into being under the Vítkov memorial. From 1784, it became the main Prague cemetery (**the Jewish, Olšany, and Vinohrady cemeteries**). Franz Kafka, among others, is buried in the Jewish Cemetery. The Olšany Cemetery is the final resting place of many famous people of modern Prague. In the 19th century, Žižkov

The television broadcasting tower in Žižkov

The Congress Centre building in Vyšehrad

was separated from Vinohrady, because Žižkov became a working class part of town, while Vinohrady became a luxurious residential area. In this part of Prague, we also find the current **Television Broadcasting Tower of Prague** in the Mahler Gardens; built during the years 1987–90, it became the new dominant feature of the town (216 m). The artist David Černý decorated it with enormous crawling infants.

NEW PRAGUE AND PRAGUE'S UNDERGROUND SYSTEM

In the recent past a number of current Prague suburbs have become part of the city. To the east of Vyšehrad and the south of Vinohrady lies **Nusle**, which may attract those interested in modern architecture. For instance,

the monumental Palace of Culture was built in 1976–81 at the foot of the Nusle Bridge, and is known today as the **Congress Centre**. This is a multi-functional, five-storey building harbouring 2,300 rooms and 5 large halls, restaurants and an underground garage. The largest hall holds 2,800 people. Housing developments lie to the south and southeast. The **Prague Underground** is one of the newest structures to bring attention to itself. From the year 1965, when the decision to build it was made, Prague's underground gradually grew and today already measures 50 km. Communists built it as a monument of its time. Newer stations are less flashy, but are well equipped with access for the disabled and other amenities. The need for grandeur was replaced by practicality.

THE HISTORY OF PRAGUE

From the 4ᵗʰ century BC   the oldest evidence of an ancient settlement in the area around Prague

5ᵗʰ/4ᵗʰ century BC   Celtic fortress at Závist u Zbraslavi, from the 2ⁿᵈ century BC the local opidum was the centre of Celts living in the Czech basin

After the year 9 BC   Marobud brought Markomans into the Czech lands (royal seat in Bubenec)

539   the Langobard king Wacho dies

5ᵗʰ–6ᵗʰ century the arrival of the Slavs

6ᵗʰ century   a Slavic culture of the Prague type with its centre at Roztoky u Prahy

8ᵗʰ century   the oldest settlement in the future Old Prague (settlement in Lesser Town)

8ᵗʰ–9ᵗʰ century the founding of Prague Castle (founded as the seat of the princedom before the year 880 – the beginning of Premyslian rule)

926   the Rotunda of St. Vitus founded in Prague Castle

973   the Prague bishopric founded

11ᵗʰ century   the rise of stone Romanesque buildings in Prague

1135–82   the Romanesque reconstruction of Prague Castle

1169   the beginning of the construction of Judith's stone bridge

1232–34   Old Town receives the rights of a city and fortifications

1257   New Town founded, later called Smaller and now Lesser Town

1310   the beginning of Luxemburg rule

1316   the last great fire of Old Town

1338   Old Town receives the right to a town hall

1344   the Prague bishopric is raised to an archbishopric; the reconstruction of St. Vitus' Cathedral begins

1348   Charles IV founds a university and New Town

1357   the construction of the stone Charles Bridge begins

1402–13   the reformer, Jan Hus, preaches at Bethlehem Chapel

1419   the first defenestration of aldermen and the beginning of the Hussite Wars

1471   the beginning of Jagiellon rule

1483   the second defenestration of Prague aldermen and the beginning of religious tolerance

1486–1502   the late Gothic reconstruction of Prague Castle

1526   the beginning of Hapsburg rule

1541   the fire of Lesser Town, Hradčany and Prague Castle

1584–1612   Prague is the residence of Emperor Rudolf II

1618   the third Prague defenestration and the beginning of the Thirty Years War

1620   the battle at Bíla hora (White Mountain) and the defeat of the Estates Uprising

1648   the Swedes plunder Rudolfs collections, Prague Castle and Lesser Town

1784   the unification of Prague's towns into the single city of Prague

1787   the premiere of Mozart's Don Giovanni

1818   the founding of the National Museum

1848   the Slovak meeting in Prague; revolution

1868   the ceremonial laying of the first stone of the National Theatre

1891   Jubilee Exhibition and the flourishing of Art Nouveau in Prague

1909–11   the cubist House of the Black Madonna is built

1918   the Czechoslovak Republic is declared

1939   Hitler occupies Prague and the protectorate of Bohemia and Moravia is announced

1945   May's Prague uprising and liberation

1948   the Communist coup

1965   the decision to build the underground (operation begins in 1974)

1968   occupation by the Warsaw Pact countries

1989   the "velvet" revolution and the renewal of democracy

1992   Prague added to UNESCO's list of monuments

1993   the division of Czechoslovakia

1999   the Czech Republic becomes a member of NATO

CULTURAL HINTS

FEBIOFEST – International film, television and video festival / January
PRAGUE WINTER – Classical music festival / January
SLOVAKIAN THEATRE IN PRAGUE – Slovakian theatre festival / February
EUROPEAN FILM DAYS – Festival of contemporary European film / March
EUROPEAN ACCORDION ORCHESTRA COMPETITION FESTIVAL / March
INTERFESTIVAL OF MAGIC – International magic competition / March
AGHARTA PRAGUE JAZZ FESTIVAL – The foremost jazz personalities and orchestras / March–December
PRAGUE WRITERS' FESTIVAL – International gathering of the authors of literary works / April
MUSICA ECUMENICA – Classical music festival / April
ONE WORLD – International human rights film festival / April
WORLD OF BOOKS IN PRAGUE – International book exhibition / May
PRAGUE SPRING – International music festival / May
KHAMORO – International Romany culture festival / May
GOLDEN PRAGUE – International television festival of musical and dance programs / May
INTERNATIONAL FOLK SONG FESTIVAL / May
WORLD PUPPET ART FESTIVAL / May – June
FESTPOL – FESTIVAL OF POLICE ORCHESTRAS AND GROUPS / June
PRAGUE DANCE – International festival of contemporary dance and motion theatre / June
MUSICA SACRA PRAGA – Religious choirs festival / June
RESPECT – Ethnic and "World Music" festival / June
SUMMER OLD MUSIC CELEBRATION – International music festival / June–July
ETHNIC FESTIVAL – The largest presentation of folk art / June–September
ORGAN SUMMER – International organ concert festival / July–August
OPERA FESTIVAL UNDER THE OPEN SKY in the Liechtenstein palace courtyard / July–August
SUMMER SHAKESPEARE CELEBRATION – a presentation of the playwright
William Shakespeare / July–September
INTERNATIONAL ORGAN FESTIVAL – Organ players concert in St. James' Basilica / August
INTERNATIONAL STRING QUARTET FESTIVAL – A festival in honour of Antonín Dvořák / August–September
YOUNG PRAGUE – International music festival / August–September
VERDI FESTIVAL – A traditional opera festival of the works of G. Verdi, the State Opera
in Prague / August–September
PRAGUE AUTUMN – International music festival / September
ST. WENCESLAS CELEBRATION – Religious music festival, ecumenically oriented / September
INTERNATIONAL JAZZ FESTIVAL / October
FOUR + FOUR DAYS IN MOTION – International motion theatre festival / October
STRING AUTUMN – Traditional classical music festival, Prague Castle / October–December
PRAGUE DAYS OF CHOIR SONGS / November
MUSICA IUDAICA – International music festival of the works of Jewish composers / November
PRAGUE GERMAN LANGUAGE THEATRE FESTIVAL – Festival of Austrian, German and
Swiss theatre groups / November
INTERNATIONAL ADVENT AND CHRISTMAS MUSIC FESTIVAL WITH THE PETER EBEN
AWARD / December
BOHUSLAV MARTINŮ FESTIVAL / December
PRAGUE CHRISTMAS – International festival of Christmas carols, traditions and advent
and Christmas music / December

A jewel of functionalism – the interior of the Müller Villa by Adolph Loos (Prague-Střešovice)

CULTURAL HINTS

Eminent galleries with permanent exhibitions:

Permanent exhibitions of the National Gallery:
Sternberg Palace – European art from antiquity to the end of the Baroque period
St. Agnes of Bohemia Convent – Medieval art in Bohemia and Central Europe
St. George's Monastery – Ancient Art Collection
Exposition Palace – Art of the 19th, 20th and 21st centuries
Zbraslav Castle – Asian Art Collections

Permanent exhibitions of the Gallery of the Capital City of Prague:
Golden Ring Building – Czech art of the 20th century
Troja Castle – Czech art of the 19th century
Bílek Villa – František Bílek studio

Prague Castle's picture gallery – Czech and European visual arts
of the 16th – 18th centuries

NOTABLE FIGURES CONNECTED WITH PRAGUE

Aostalli de Sala, Ulrico (1525–1597) – Renaissance builder and architect of Prague Castle

Appollinaire, Guillaume (1880–1918) – Poet; a visit to Prague became the inspiration for the prose work The Prague Walker

Barrande, Joachim (1799–1883) – geologist and palaeontologist; the Barrandov quarter of Prague is named for him

Beethoven, Ludwig van (1770–1827) – composer; in 1796 organised a number of public performances in Prague

Bolzano, Bernard (1781–1848) – Mathematician and philosopher, the forefather of modern logic

Brahe, Tycho (1546–1601) – Astronomer, worked in the court of Rudolph II, buried in Týn Cathedral

Braun, Matthias Bernard (1684–1738) – Sculptor, author of sculptures on Charles's Bridge (St. Lutgarde)

Brod, Max (1884–1968) – Writer, published writings of Franz Kafka, promoted the works of Leoš Janáček

Brokoff, Ferdinand Maxmilián (1688–1731) – Sculptor, author of sculptures on Charles Bridge, (e. g. sculpture of St. Barbora [Barbara])

Tchaikovsky, Peter Ilyich (1840–1893) – Composer, conducted his works during several visits to Prague

Čapek, Karel (1890–1938) – Writer; e. g. R. U. R., Krakatit, White Malady, The Mother

Dienzenhofer, Kilián Ignác (1689–1751) – Baroque architect; e.g. the church of St. Nicholas

Dvořák, Antonín (1841–1904) – Composer, director of the school of music in Prague; e.g. Slavonic dance, Rusalka

Einstein, Albert (1879–1955) – Physicist; professor at the German university of Prague from 1911–1912

Hašek, Jaroslav (1883–1923) – Writer; e. g. The Good Soldier Švejk during the First World War

Hollar, Václav [Wenceslas] (1607–1677) – Engraver and draftsman, author of engravings, vistas, hand-drawn maps and portraits

Hus, Jan (approx. 1371–1415) – Religious reformer; preacher in the Bethlehem Chapel (1402–1412)

Ibrahím Íbn Jakúb (died sometime after 970) – Jewish merchant and diplomat, produced the first record of Prague

Kafka, Franz (1883–1924) – Writer; e.g. The Trial, The Castle, Amerika *wrote in German*

Kubelík, Rafael (1914–1996) – Conductor and composer; conductor of the Czech Philharmonic Orchestra (1942–1948)

Liszt, Franz (1811–1886) – Composer, conductor and pianist; organised many concerts in Prague

Mahler, Gustav (1860–1911) – Composer and conductor; conductor at the German theatre ("Německé divadlo") of Prague (1885–1886)

Maultbertsch, Franz Anton (1724–1796) – Baroque painter; author of ceiling frescoes at the Premonstratensian monastery in Strahov

Matthias of Arras (1290–1352) – builder and architect; began the construction of St. Vitus's Cathedral

Morstadt, Vincenc (1802–1875) – Painter and draftsman; author of Prague vistas

Mozart, Wolfgang Amadeus (1756–1791) – Composer; launched the premier of the opera Don Giovanni in Stavovské Theatre

Myslbek, Josef Václav (1848–1922) – Sculptor; author of the St. Wenceslas monument on Wenceslas Square

Negrelli, Alois (1799–1858) – Railway engineer and builder; author of the unique Negrelli viaduct

Nestroy, Johann Nepomuk (1801–1862) – Playwright; performed several times in Prague in the 1840s

Parléř, Petr (1332–1399) – Architect and sculptor of middle pointed style; builder of St. Vitus's Cathedral

Plečnik, Josip (1872–1957) – Architect, led repairs on Prague Castle from 1920–1931

Rilke, Rainer Maria (1875–1926) – poet and writer; native of Prague

Seifert, Jaroslav (1901–1986) – Poet and Nobel Prize winner for Literature

Šaljapin, Fjodor (1873–1938) – Russian opera singer; appeared at the National Theatre in the 1920s and 30s

Škréta, Karel (1610–1674) – Baroque painter; among other works, decorated the church of St. Nicholas and the church Our Lady Before Týn (Matky Boží před Týnem)

de Vries, Adrian (circa 1545–1626) – court sculptor for Rudolf II; among other works, statues for Valdštejn (Wallenstein) Palace

Weber, Carl Maria von (1786–1826) – Composer and conductor; opera director at Estates Theatre (1813–1816)

Werfel, Franz (1890–1945) – Writer; e. g. Graduate Convention, House of Sorrow, The Forty Days of Musa Dagh

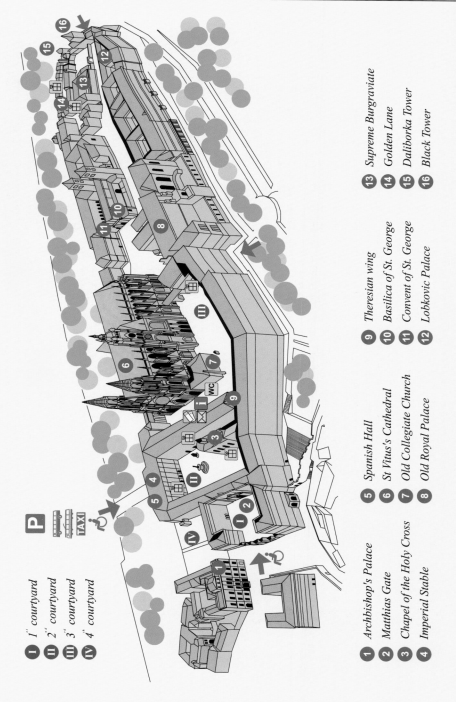

1 1ˢᵗ courtyard
II 2ⁿᵈ courtyard
III 3ʳᵈ courtyard
IV 4ᵗʰ courtyard

1 Archbishop's Palace
2 Mathias Gate
3 Chapel of the Holy Cross
4 Imperial Stable
5 Spanish Hall
6 St Vitus's Cathedral
7 Old Collegiate Church
8 Old Royal Palace
9 Theresian wing
10 Basilica of St. George
11 Convent of St. George
12 Lobkovic Palace
13 Supreme Burgraviate
14 Golden Lane
15 Daliborka Tower
16 Black Tower

The Monastic Brewery Strahov is located near the Prague Castle within premises of the Strahov Monastery, which was established in 1140. The first written records of the brewery are dated to the break of the 13th and 14th century. Nowadays the brewery functions as a restaurant's mini-brewery producing own Sv. Norbert beer. Overall abacity of 370 places is divided into 3 specific premises, which are usable in many ways depending on customer's demands. The brewery offer, next to delicious beer, also Old-Bohemian cuisine in stylish interiors and ambience during suppers is enhanced by live music performances.

Klášterní pivovar Strahov
Strahovské nádvoří 301
Praha 1, 118 00
tel: +420 233 353 155
fax: +420 233 355 690
e-mail:
zuzana.pivovar@seznam.cz
www.klasterni-pivovar.cz

JAN BECHER ⊕ MUZEUM

Exkurse &
Degustace

OPEN DAILY 9:00am - 5:00pm

   VISIT our fascinating collection of bottles, labels
and drinking cups, then tour our great distillery
to see where **BECHEROVKA** is made.
Let us show you around the historic
cellars and enjoy the unique taste
of our famous herbal liqueur.

Karlovarská
Becherovka
1807

T.G.MASARYKA 57 - 360 76 KARLOVY VARY
CZECH REPUBLIC
TEL.: +420 353 170 156, FAX.: +420 353 229 421
E-mail: muzeum@janbecher.cz, www.janbecher.cz

RESTAURANT U MODRÉ RŮŽE
(THE BLUE ROSE)

Welcome to the 15th century

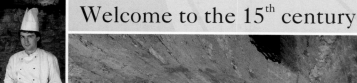

Czech and international experience gastronomy
Moravian, French, Spanish, Italian and Chilean wines
Intimate, exclusive 15th century setting
Piano music every evening
VISA, AMEX, DC, EC/MC, JCB

Tel: +420/224 225 873, +420/224 222 634, +420/224 222 636, fax: + 420/224 222 623
www.umodreruze.cz, restaurant@umodreruze.cz

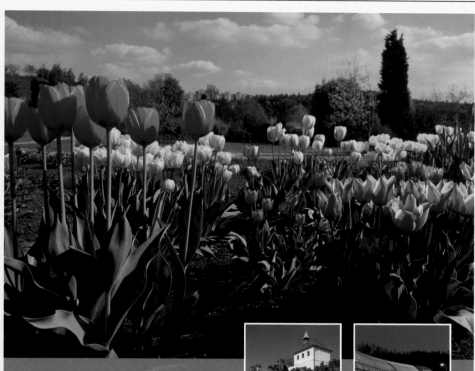

Enter the Realm of Plants

A green oasis situated in a charming place in Prague Troja offers you an unusual encounter with the world of plants. You will find here extensive outdoor expositions, a Japanese garden as well as a National Heritage vineyard with the Chapel of St. Clara, a vineyard house dating from the 17th century and a wine collection. The world of exotic plants is represented by a tropical greenhouse named Fata Morgana built straight into a natural rock. Come and see one of the most beautiful places in Prague.

Opening times:

March, October	9:00 – 17:00
April	9:00 – 18:00
May – September	9:00 – 19:00
November – February	9:00 – 16:00

Outdoor exhibit areas and St. Clara vineyard:

15th March – 31st October	Daily
1st November – 15th March	Tuesday – Sunday
Greenhouse Fata Morgana:	
all year-round	Tuesday – Sunday

Prague Botanical Garden

Nádvorní 134, Praha 7 - Troja
www.botanicka.cz

Getting there: from the subway station Holesovicke Nadrazi by bus No 112 to stop Zoo or Botanicka zahrada.

Botanická zahrada Praha

Anton Richa - Czech composer,
b. 1770
wrote famous book on harmony